Seeking Singleness

DYLAN POWELL

Scriptures is taken from the KING JAMES VERSION (KJV): KING JAMES VERSION, public domain.

Dedication

I would like to dedicate this book to God. It is He who brought me from sorrow to satisfaction in my singleness. He was the one who provided me with the burden to reach out to young, single men and women. "Seeking Singleness" is based on Scripture and the very words of God. Thank you for your Word. Thank you for your Cross. Thank you for my Life. Thank you for this Opportunity.

Table of Contents

Self-Evaluation of Singleness

As you read through these chapters, reflect upon your heart and answer the following questions (there is no right or wrong answer. This is about what you got from the book):

Chapters 1-4:

1. What is your state of singleness?

2. What sin do you battle in singleness?

3. What scars do you have from singleness?

4. What is the difference between solitude and loneliness?

Chapters 5-6:

1. How can you have surety in your singleness?

2. What two major factors are a result of your sincerity?

Self-Evaluation of Singleness

As you read through these chapters, reflect upon your heart and answer the following questions (there is no right or wrong answer. This is about what you got from the book):

Chapters 7-9:

1. How can you surrender to God in singleness of heart?

2. In what ways can you be a better servant of Christ?

3. What things do you need to sacrifice to be a better servant?

Chapters 10-11:

1. How can you be satisfied in your state of singleness?

2. What is the solution to singleness?

Introduction

I have found three instances in the Bible where the word "singleness" is used:

> *"Servants, obey in all things your masters according to the flesh; not with eyeservice, as menpleasers; but in <u>singleness of heart</u>, fearing God"* (Colossians 3:22).

> *"Servants, be obedient to them that are your masters according to the flesh, with fear and trembling, <u>in singleness of your heart</u>, as unto Christ"* (Ephesians 6:5).

> *"And they, continuing daily with one accord in the temple, and breaking bread from house to house, did eat their meat with gladness and <u>singleness of heart</u>"* (Acts 2:46).

Look carefully at these three verses and let's compare them. Every time that you see the word singleness mentioned, it follows with "of heart." This shows us that there is a direct correlation between singleness and the heart. You cannot experience singleness without a heart for God; likewise, you cannot have a heart for God without first experiencing true singleness with God.

"Singleness" (according to Webster's American Dictionary of the English Language, 1828) is defined in two ways: 1. The state of being one only or separate from all others; the opposite of doubleness, complication, or multiplicity. 2. Simplicity; sincerity; purity of mind or purpose; freedom from duplicity; as singleness of belief; singleness of heart.

"Single" (according to Webster's American Dictionary of the English Language, 1828), in relation to a person, is defined as: 1. unmarried; as a single man; a single woman. 2. Alone; having no companion or assistant. Nowhere does the Bible use the word single in relation to a person's relationship status; however, we can see the principle of being single in I Corinthians 7:8. *"I say therefore to the unmarried and widows, it is good for them if they abide even as I."* How then are we to be "Seeking Singleness?"

The word seek is found many times in the Bible; note several instances that I have found:

> *"When thou saidst, <u>Seek</u> ye my face; my heart said unto thee, Thy face, LORD, will I <u>seek</u>"* (Psalm 27:8).

> *"But if from thence thou shalt <u>seek</u> the LORD thy God, thou shalt find him, if thou <u>seek</u> him with all thy heart and with all thy soul"* (Deuteronomy 4:29).

> *"And he did evil, because he prepared not his heart to <u>seek</u> the LORD"* (II Chronicles 12:14).

> *"Glory ye in his holy name: let the heart of them rejoice that <u>seek</u> the LORD"* (I Chronicles 16:10; Psalm 105:3).

> *"Blessed are they that keep his testimonies, and that <u>seek</u> him with the whole heart"* (Psalm 119:2).

> *"And ye shall <u>seek</u> me, and find men, when ye shall search for me with all your heart"* (Jeremiah 29:13).

> *"And I gave my heart to <u>seek</u> and search out by wisdom concerning all things that are done under heaven"* (Ecclesiastes 1:13).

Not only do we find a <u>connection</u> between singleness and the heart, but we find the <u>condition</u> that our heart must be in to seek singleness. We must be "seeking singleness within our heart."

Singleness is so much more than a relationship status. Quite contrarily to what the world believes, singleness is not about your distance from the opposite sex, it is about your nearness to God.

Chapter 1:
States of Singleness

While my greatest burden and desire is to reach those who are single, this book is not subject only to single people. There are several "states of singleness" which Paul describes in I Corinthians chapter seven (his epistle to the Church of Corinth). The chapter begins with, *"Now concerning the things whereof ye wrote unto me."* Apparently, the people of Corinth had many of the same questions and situations that we have in relationships today. Throughout the entire chapter, Paul, with the Lord's guidance, will <u>seek</u> to answer these many different questions. Who can say that the Bible, which was penned over 2,000 years ago, is not relevant to our society today?

In verse eight, Paul begins with those who are single. *"I say therefore to the unmarried and widows, it is good for them if they abide even as I."* I believe when the word <u>single</u> is presented in our culture, many people think only of young people who have not married or are not in a relationship. We find that widow or widowers (those who have lost their spouse due to death) are also mentioned as part of Paul's main audience.

In reference to widows, Paul writes, *"The wife is bound by the law as long as her husband liveth; but if her husband be dead, she is at liberty to be married to whom she will; only in the Lord. But she is happier if she so abide, after my judgment: and I think also that I have the Spirit of God."* Although a widow is no longer bound by the covenant of marriage, Paul encourages her to embrace and "seek singleness" in the midst of her single state.

In verse eleven, Paul makes reference to people who are separated, *"But and if she depart, let her remain unmarried or be reconciled to her husband: and let not the husband put away his wife."* While we can put divorced people into this general category, understand that God's intention for marriage is NEVER divorce.

The Bible says in Matthew 19:3-6,

"The Pharisees also came unto him, tempting him, and saying unto him, Is it lawful for a man to put away his wife for every cause? And he answered and said unto them, Have ye not read, that he which made them at the beginning made them male and female, And said, For this cause shall man leave father and mother, and shall cleave to his wife: and they twain shall be one flesh? Wherefore they are no more twain, but one flesh. What therefore God hath joined together, let not man put asunder."

Notice the question asked versus the answer given. At first, Jesus did not deal with their original question. The answer did not need to be directed towards divorce, it needed to be directed to God's intention for marriage.

This answer was not enough to satisfy the hearts and minds of the Pharisees. They continued their questioning, *"Why did Moses then command to give a writing of divorcement, and to put her away?"* The Pharisees further tempted Jesus by attempting to trap Him in His own words. If God's intention for marriage was one man and one woman for life, then why do we have divorce? I present to you that it is the same reason we have sin in the world.

Genesis 1:31 records what God said after He created all things. *"And God saw every thing that he had made, and, behold, it was very good."* When the Bible says, *"it was very good,"* it means that God created everything complete and perfect in Himself. God's intention for the world was to be perfect; however, we find that the evil hearts of man would distort His intention. We know through the record of "the fall of man," recorded in Genesis chapter three, it was man who ushered sin into the world, not God. God is not the author of sin. This is the same for divorce!

Divorce was never intended by God, it is the result of man's hardened heart that Moses had to deal with the issue. Notice Jesus's response to the Pharisees question. *"He saith unto them, Moses because of the <u>hardness of your hearts</u> suffered you to put away your wives: but from the beginning it was not so."* Pay attention to the

14

root of divorce. It was not God. It was not Moses. It was not a commandment. The root was the *"hardness of [their] hearts."* It is not ironic that Christ directs their attention right back to the state of their heart.

When dealing with singleness, I am not only talking about the state of your relationship with people, but the state of your relationship with God. Without the hardness of man's heart, divorce would have never been a thing!

Now is a good time to point out the disciples' response to Jesus's answer to the Pharisees. Verse ten says, *"His disciples say unto him, If the case of the man be so with his wife, it is not good to marry."* Many people would try to take this verse and claim that the Word of God contradicts itself. How? Genesis 2:18 states, *"And the Lord God said, It is not good that the man should be alone; I will make him an help meet for him."* Now, if we just skim over these two verses it might sound as if God has contradicted Himself. We can be assured that just as God is not the author of sin, He is not the author of confusion. God declared that Adam's solitude was not good. Many say people who remain single are living outside of God's will for their life. However, notice God created *"the man."* God said that it was not good for Adam to be alone. God did not say, it is not good that all men should be alone. God does not create all men with the same gifts, purposes, or desires. God saw fit that Adam needed to relate to one who was meet, or complimentary for him. God did not only see the need, but He sought to fill the need.

Jesus's response to the disciples was,

"But he said unto them, All men cannot receive this saying, save they to whom it is given. For there are some eunuchs, which were so born from their mother's womb: and there are some eunuchs, which were made eunuchs of men: and there be some eunuchs, which have made themselves eunuchs for the kingdom of heaven's sake. He that is able to receive it, let him receive it."

Here we will take the PRINCIPLE of a Eunuch who voluntarily abstained from marriage in order to devote himself fully to God.

15

Being capable of doing such is a gift from God as described in I Corinthians 7:7, *"But every man hath his proper gift of God, one after this manner, and another after that."* Contrary to what the world might think, being single is a gift from God. It is in this state, God allows us to seek singleness to its fullest!

When we break down God's intentions for our life, we will find two different categories: either God blesses us with the gift of remaining single or He blesses us with the gift of marriage. Paul describes the characteristics of these two categories, In I Corinthians 7:32-34,

> *"But I would have you without carefulness. He that is unmarried careth for the things that belong to the Lord, how he may please the Lord: But he that is married careth for the things that are of the world, how he may please his wife. There is difference also between a wife and a virgin. The unmarried woman careth for the things of the Lord, that she may be both holy both in body and in spirit: but she that is married careth for the things of the world, how she may please her husband."*

He distinguishes between those who are married and those who are single. Regardless of the state you are in, God wants to fill your need just as he filled Adam's. God led Paul not only to instruct the ways of the unmarried, but also to those who are widows, married, separated, divorced, and virgins. How can we seek singleness when we are not single?

Remember, singleness does not define the state of your relationship, it defines the state of your heart toward God. No matter the state of singleness that you fit into, you can seek singleness.

In verse twelve, Paul adds, "but to the rest speak I..." Any group who he has not yet included, he includes here. Singleness to God is more than just for single people!

Chapter 2:
Sin in Singleness

In chapter five, we find Paul's reasoning behind his epistle to the Church in Corinth. *"It is reported commonly that there is fornication among you, and such fornication as is not so much as named among the Gentiles..."* Corinth had a carnal, or Christ-likeness, problem. What we must not miss is that many of their carnality problems were rooted in their sexual sin. As Christians, we must seek to avoid all occasions of sin and flee from all fleshly lusts. One of the greatest attacks on the Church today is the temptation of sexual sin. When looking at sexual sin, we often take the root word sex and assume it to be the only issue. Sexual sin comes in many different forms other than just sex.

The first issue Paul deals with is the sexual sin of fornication. Fornication is the incontinence or lewdness of unmarried people. In a simple man's definition, fornication is "sex outside of marriage."

In the Bible, fornication is also used for the word adultery. Adultery is the unfaithfulness of any married person to the marriage bed. The simple man's definition of adultery would be "sex outside of your marriage." Single people commit fornication, married people commit adultery.

I Corinthians chapter seven begins with these words, *"Now concerning the things whereof ye wrote unto me: It is good for a man not to touch a woman."* It amazes me that over 2,000 years ago, men and women had the same questions about relationships that we still have today. Even more jaw dropping is that over 2,000 years ago God gave us the answers in His Word. We have all the answers, but we still seek them from the world. The world doesn't have the answers that we need, God does.

So often we raise our young men to believe it is alright to look as long as you don't touch; however, this is contrary to God's way! Men must neither touch, nor look upon a woman, so as to provoke lustful inclinations. What did Jesus say about this matter when he was teaching on the mountain? *"Ye have heard that it was said by them of old time, Thou shalt not commit adultery: But I say unto you, That whosoever looketh on a woman to lust after her hath committed adultery with her already in his heart"* (Matthew 5:27-28). I've always said, "sin is sin, it doesn't matter how thin." How many times, like the Pharisees, do we think that we are righteous because we have not committed adultery or fornication?

Sexual sin does not begin whenever we <u>touch</u> something we shouldn't, it begins when we <u>desire</u> something we shouldn't. Where did Jesus say that a person first committed the sin of adultery? *"In his heart."* Sexual sin begins in the wicked desires of the heart, builds up through the lust of our eyes, and at last is fulfilled in submission through touch. All sin is rooted in the heart. This is why we must seek singleness of heart toward God!

To better understand the dangers of sexual sin in a believer's life, let's examine the life of someone who fell into it. The most familiar record that comes to my mind is that of David and Bathsheba in II Samuel chapter eleven. While David and Bathsheba were not single, I believe we can gain great truth about sexual sin from them.

The Satisfaction of Sin

II Samuel 11:2 reads, *"And it came to pass in an eveningtide, that David arose from off his bed, and walked upon the roof of the king's house: and from the roof he saw a woman washing herself."* At this point, David had not yet sinned. He simply walked on top of his roof and saw something that was out in the world. As Christians, it is not hard for us to walk out of our homes and see sin all around us. In fact, it is not hard for us to stay at home and see sin on our phones, televisions, magazines, etc. However, just because evil is in the world, doesn't mean that we are obligated to sin or excused from sin.

Verse two continues, *"And the woman was very beautiful to look upon."* David didn't just <u>see</u> her, but he <u>looked</u> upon her. As a Christian, if you <u>see</u> sin, then you should <u>separate</u> from sin. If you continue to <u>look</u> upon it, then you will begin to <u>lust</u> upon it. After

David saw her, he didn't separate from her. His eyes began to <u>stay</u> on her and sin creeped in. Satan always begins with the satisfaction of sin. He puts things before us that look pleasing to our eyes. Naturally, men are pleased by what they see and women are pleased by what they hear. Do not allow Satan to tempt you where your weakness is. Pray for strength to stay away from the satisfaction of sin.

The Secrecy of Sin

David's sin began with the lust of his eyes; however, it was not finished yet. Verse three says, *"And David sent and inquired after the woman."* When we allow sin to creep into our hearts through our eyes, we cannot be satisfied with just looking. David wanted to know more about this sin because it was so pleasing to his eyes. Yet he did not want others to know about the temptation that he had fallen into. He <u>secretly</u> sent messengers to inquire more about Bathsheba. When sin looks good, smells good, or sounds good, then you will be tempted to taste, touch, and take it!

Do you remember when young David slayed Goliath? How did he respond at that time? He publicly announced that he had done the Lord's work, and openly gave God the glory for it. Now we find that same David, several years later, who is quietly doing Satan's work, and secretly attempting to cover up his own sin.

In II Samuel 12:12, God proclaims to David through the prophet Nathan, "For thou didst it <u>secretly</u>." We may think we are doing a good job of keeping our sin secret from the world, but there is always One who knows even the deepest of secrets.

The Submission to Sin

Pay close attention to the down-hill spiral that sexual sin has in a person's life. Verse four says, *"and David sent messengers, and took her; and she came in unto him, and he lay with her; for she was purified from her uncleanness: and she returned unto her house."* What began as <u>looking upon sin</u>, soon turned into <u>submission to sin</u>.

19

What is the answer to fleeing from submission to sin? Paul writes, *"Flee Fornication. Every sin that a man doeth is without the body; but he that committeth fornication sinneth against his own body. What? Know ye not that your body is the temple of the Holy Ghost which is in you, which ye have of God, and ye are not your own? For ye are bought with a price: therefore glorify God in your body, and in your spirit, which are God's"* (I Corinthians 6:18-20). Murder, stealing, lying, cursing, etc. are all sins that are without your body and are committed towards others. They start on the inside and they come out through your eyes, mouth, or actions. Paul explained that sexual sin is quite different. Fornication, adultery, homosexuality, incest, pornography, and masturbation are all sins that you commit towards your own body. Whether you realize it or not, you are doing more damage to yourself than you are doing to others with sexual sin.

Maybe you didn't expect me to name some of the things I listed above. Maybe your heart was just pierced because you realize you are actively partaking in one of these as a Christian. Maybe you didn't realize that some of these are actually sin. May I remind you that I Thessalonians 5:22 says, *"abstain from all appearance of evil."* The Bible instructs us to abstain from the very appearance of evil. That is ALL evil! Maybe you have hardened your hearts to God and you don't want to give up one of these sins. As Christians, we all struggle. You are not to be ashamed with what you struggle with, you are to give it to God and allow him to help you through it victoriously.

In I Corinthians 3:16-17, Paul wrote, *"Know ye not that ye are the temple of God, and that the Spirit of God dwelleth in you? If any man defile the temple of God, him shall God destroy; for the temple of God is holy, which temple ye are."* We should see the importance of abstaining from all sexual sin in this verse alone. If you are saved, then your body is the temple of the Holy Spirit. Why would you ever want to defile your body and use it for an occasion of sexual sin against God? If you defile your temple, the Word says that God shall destroy you!

In I Corinthians 6:15, Paul writes, *"Know ye not that your bodies are the members of Christ? Shall I then take the members of*

Christ, and make them the members of an harlot? God forbid." This verse shows the impact of sin in the lives of others. Not only are you to protect your body for your own service to the Lord, but for the members of the whole body of Christ. Use your body to glorify God in holiness, not to defile him in sinfulness!

The Self-Covering of Sin

I am not concerned with knowing what sexual sin you may be battling today; whether it's homosexuality, pornography, masturbation, or any other unnamed. However, I am concerned with knowing what you plan to do about this problem. In II Samuel 11:14-17, we see how David handled his sexual sin:

> *"And it came to pass in the morning, that David wrote a letter to Joab, and sent it by the hand of Uriah. And he wrote in this letter, saying, Set ye Uriah in the forefront of the hottest battle, and retire ye from him, that he may be smitten, and die. And it came to pass, when Joab observed the city, that he assigned Uriah unto a place where he knew that valiant men were. And the men of the city went out, and fought with Joab: and there fell some of the people of the servants of David; and Uriah the Hittite died also."*

One simple sin must always be covered and secured with another. The beginnings of sin are therefore to be dreaded; for who knows where they will end? What began as lust of the eyes, soon led to the murder of a man. How quick can sin escalate in your life?

Rather than giving his sin to God and asking forgiveness, David decided to try and cover it himself. First, he called Uriah home from the battlefield and attempted to convince him to go home to his wife. Once that attempt failed, David made Uriah drunk; however, he still would not go home. After two failed attempts, he decided to take the last resort and have Uriah killed. Notice David sent Uriah's death sentence by his very own hands. What a change sexual sin can make in a person's life!

Your sexual sin doesn't just affect you, it affects all those around you. Whose lives were affected by David's sin? First of all,

Bathsheba, because her husband was murdered. Not only did Uriah die, but *"some of the people of the servants of David"* died also. Innocent people's lives were ruined as the result of one man's sin. Don't let your sexual sin go on any longer; you do not know who or what will be hurt by it.

In II Samuel 12:1-12, Nathan exposed David's sin by the parable of the ewe lamb. Verse twelve says, "For thou didst it secretly: but I will do this thing before all Israel, and before the sun." What you try to cover, God will uncover. But what you uncover, God will cover.

The Self-Evaluation of Sin

If God is dealing with your heart about some sexual sin in your life, I encourage you to pray to God at this very moment. I John 1:9 says, *"If we confess our sins, he is faithful and just to forgive us our sins, and to cleanse us from all unrighteousness."* Confess your sin before Him, ask for His forgiveness, and commit to turn away from it.

Among young boys and girls, I believe the most popular sexual sins are pornography and masturbation. I believe this due to the simple fact of how accessible they are. To say that only young people deal with pornography and masturbation would be a great lie. How do you expect your children to be pure if you cannot be pure? How will you trust your children with a phone if you cannot trust yourself?

Among young men and women, I believe that the most popular sexual sins are pornography, masturbation, homosexuality, and fornication. Those young children who began to watch pornography and masturbate are most likely those same young men and women who are still addicted to it on a weekly, if not daily basis. As a child develops into a young adult, he is tempted with taking hold of sexual sin rather than just looking at it. The product of pornography and masturbation in the life of a child will be fornication in the life of a young adult. The product of fornication in the life of a young adult will be adultery in the life of an adult.

Young people are being told by their peers that they are awkward if they are single. They're being told that if they haven't had sex by the age of sixteen, then something is wrong with them. They're being told that if they do not make sexual jokes towards women, then they are not cool. They're being told that if they do not watch pornography, then they are missing out. They're being told that if they do not masturbate, then they are not normal. Young men, can I tell you that those things aren't the qualities of "just a boy," they are the qualities of a sinner. We need to stop excusing sin in the lives of young men by saying, "boys will be boys." Boys will be the men that you raise and train them to be!

Today, everything that we watch portrays sexual sin. Everything that we listen to portrays sexual sin. Every place we go portrays sexual sin. Saddest of all is many Christians lives portray sexual sin! I Corinthians 5:9-10 says, *"I wrote unto you in an epistle not to company with fornicators: Yet not altogether with the fornicators of this world, or with the covetous, or extortioners, or with idolaters; for then must ye needs go out of the world."* In a world filled with fornication, adultery, pornography, and masturbation, we must remain separated from it. This causes me to reflect upon the importance of what God commanded in the book of Romans, *"be not conformed to this world."*

We have established that sexual sin is sin against God and unto your own body. We have examined several different types of sexual sins; however, at its core, what is sexual sin? I Corinthians 7:4 says, *"The wife hath not power of her own body, but the husband: and likewise also the husband hath not power of his own body, but the wife."* Most people assume that since the husband and wife are in control of each other's body in marriage, then they have control of their own body when they are single. May I contradict; your body should never belong to yourself, it ought to belong to God. Not only are you called to give your heart to God in singleness, but you are commanded to give your body to Him in singleness!

I Corinthians 6:20 says, *"For ye are bought with a price: therefore glorify God in your body, and in your spirit, which are God's."* If you have given your life to Christ, then you must give your body to Him. If you have given your body to Christ, then you

---

23

have a greater responsibility to care for it. It is God who has given you your body in the first place; therefore, you must give back to Him what he has graciously given to you. Would it be fair to give God a dysfunctional body after He has given you a fully functional body?

Sexual activity in a Christians life is only intended for marriage; the covenant between a married man and woman. Genesis 2:24 says, *"Therefore shall a man leave his father and his mother, and shall cleave unto his wife: and they shall be one flesh."* Anything outside of marriage that smells, tastes, looks, feels, or even resembles sexual activity is sexual sin. I included masturbation as sexual sin because it distorts God's intended purpose for your body. I believe many young people question such issues as masturbation because they aren't named directly in the Bible. While the word may not be there, the principle is. I am convicted and convinced that these very things are all sexual sin. I believe if you will give your heart to singleness in the Lord that he will reveal the same to you.

We must take a stand against sexual sin in the lives of ourselves and our children. Now is the time to talk to your children. If you don't talk to them about the dangers of sexual sin, then someone else will talk to them about the pleasures of sexual sin. If you don't demonstrate a life of godliness before them, then someone else will demonstrate a life of worldliness before them.

Is our real problem sexual sin? No, but sexual sin is a result of our real problem. II Chronicles 12:14 says, *"And he did evil, because he prepared not his heart to seek the LORD."* Get away from sins of the heart and draw near to singleness of heart! Prepare your hearts now.

Chapter 3:
Scars of Singleness

Where there <u>was</u> sin, there <u>will be</u> scars. What I have found in my very short life is, in every state of singleness there are scars. We have all looked back to the different states we were once in, and have regrets about them. There are some things we wish we could take away, and other things that we wish we could add to.

There are some scars that I am sure that I have no answers for because I have never been through those situations. However, I can tell you with full assurance, that God's Word has the answers for the deepest scars in your life. There are some scars that I am not aware of how deep they actually are, but I can assure you that no wound is too deep for Christ to heal. Psalm 147:3 says, *"He healeth the broken in heart, and bindeth up their wounds."*

If we continue looking at the sin of David and Bathsheba, we know that the story didn't end with Uriah the Hittite's death. We can find two more key points from the effects of sin and the scars of singleness.

The Sorrow of Scars

II Samuel 11:26 says, *"And when the wife of Uriah heard that Uriah her husband was dead, she mourned for her husband."* Sin <u>always</u> leads to sorrow. The pleasure of sin always lasts a season, but will soon leave you in a lower state than before. Think about how much David worked to take hold of his sin. He watched Bathsheba upon the roof, he lusted over her as she bathed, he sent and inquired after her, then he sent messengers to retrieve her. He did all of this, yet we find the pleasure of his sin only lasted one night. Read verse four, *"And she came in unto him, and he lay with her; for she was purified from her uncleanness: and she returned unto her house."* He finally got the thing he had most desired and labored for, but he only had it for a few hours. Satan has a way with words to make you think the pleasure of your sin will last forever;

however, sin is short lived. What is not short lived, though, are the effects of sin. Sorrow is one effect of sin that no one can escape.

We have recorded the sorrow and mourning of Bathsheba over her husband's death, but what about the family of Uriah. What about the families of *"some of the people of the servants of David"* who were also slain. This is why I place great emphasis on sin in my life. If you don't care about the effects that sin will have on you, then at least take others into consideration.

We also see that the remainder of David's life was marked by sorrow. What once was <u>sin in his walk</u> with the Lord, is now a <u>scar in his way</u> with the Lord.

We find David's realization and repentance of sin in II Samuel 12:13. *"And David said unto Nathan, I have sinned against the LORD. And Nathan said unto David, The LORD also hath put away thy sin; thou shalt not die."* Isn't it amazing that the Lord forgave him of this great sin! In Hebrews 10:17 the Bible says, *"And their sins and iniquities will I remember no more."* Although David's sin was completely forgiven by God, he had not escaped the consequences from it. While God forgets, we will remember. Satan always seeks to remind us of the sin of our past through the scars of our present.

Let's look at one more sorrow of sin that was brought to David. II Samuel 12:14 says, *"Howbeit, because by this deed thou hast given great occasion to the enemies of the LORD to blaspheme, the child also that is born unto thee shall surely die."* After reading this account of David's sin, many people assume that the conception of the child was the consequence of his sin; however, this is far from the case. It would be losing the child that was his true consequence. Every child that is conceived, even in sin, is a blessing from the Lord. We must remember, the Lord can take away from us just as he gives unto us. Oh, the sorrow comes from sin!

The Separation of Scars

II Samuel chapter eleven ends with, *"But the thing that David had done displeased the LORD."* Sin causes separation in

---

your life. Now, I do not mean that if you sin then you are separated from salvation. I have always said it like this, "our relationship is never broke, but our fellowship often chokes." While nothing *"shall be able to separate us from the love of God, which is in Christ Jesus our Lord"* (Romans 8:39), we can distance ourselves from a right relationship with God because of our sin. My relationship with the Lord can never be broken, but I can take my fellowship with the Lord and put a choke on it because of the unconfessed sin in my life.

The Bible says in 51:9-12,

"Hide thy face from my sins, and blot out all mine iniquities. Create in me a clean heart, O God; and renew a right spirit within me. Cast me not away from thy presence; and take not thy holy spirit from me. Restore unto me the joy of thy salvation; and uphold me with thy free spirit."

Pay attention to the word heart. In the introduction of this book, we placed special attention on the heart. If we are going to seek singleness, then we must have a clean heart. Where do we get a clean heart? We get our <u>clean heart</u> after we have come to God with our <u>contrite heart</u>.

Notice the words *"and take not thy holy spirit from me."* God's work through the Holy Spirit was different in David's day than it is today. The Holy Spirit's work in the Old Testament was that of empowerment, meaning that God empowered believers at certain times to complete His divine purpose. Since Christ had not yet come and died, been buried, risen, and ascended, the Holy Spirit could not play the role of indwelling believers. Jesus said in John 16:7, *"Nevertheless I tell you the truth; It is expedient for you that I go away: for if I go not away, the Comforter will not come unto you; but if I depart, I will send him unto you."* David's plea to God did not mean that Christians can lose their salvation. David remembered how the Spirit of God had departed from King Saul because of his sin, and he did not want God to do the same to him. David asked God to restore *"the joy"* of his salvation. I believe sin causes us to lose the joy we ought to have in our salvation.

—

The Shapes of Scars

No scars look exactly alike, even if your experiences are similar. Sin has a different impact in every person's life, but the results are always the same: Sorrow and Separation. Let's examine a few different shapes of scars that come from being single.

Maybe you are single and you have never been in a relationship with anyone. Maybe you have feelings of not being loved or wanted by anyone. Maybe you have been praying for God's guidance in a relationship, but it doesn't feel like he is sending anyone your way. Seek Singleness.

Maybe you are single because you have just found your way out of a relationship. Maybe you are brokenhearted and you don't know what to do now. Maybe you are wondering how God could ever give you something better than what you once had. Maybe you are having a hard time adjusting to being single. Seek Singleness.

Maybe you are a widow or widower, because your spouse has recently died. Maybe you feel completely lost without that person. Maybe you have not given your situation to the Lord. Maybe you lost your loved one due to an accident, disease, or suffering, and you have grown a hardened heart toward God through this situation. Seek Singleness.

Maybe you are divorced and now you are feeling the grief and heartache from that decision. As a preacher of the Word of God, I will never *excuse* divorce in any way, form, fashion, or circumstance. It is not your pastor's place, or any other person's place, to excuse your circumstance either. This ought to be between you and the Lord. You search out the scriptures that the Lord has given. You bow down your face before God in prayer and ask Him for guidance. I can tell you one thing for sure, regardless if you agree or not; it is <u>best</u> to remain as you are. In every single state of a person, Paul encourages him/her to remain as they are. Being divorced doesn't mean your life is over, you are not loved, or you cannot be used by God. Being divorced means that you need to do like everyone else… Seek Singleness.

Maybe you are a virgin who is saving yourself for marriage. Maybe you have committed your life and your body to the Lord. Maybe you have been picked on because you boldly stand and proclaim it. Maybe you are beginning to have temptations of sexual sin. Seek Singleness.

Maybe you are not a virgin and you wish that you could take your mistakes back. Ask for forgiveness and make a commitment to God that from here on out you will live a sexually pure life. It is never too late to give your life and body to the Lord. Seek Singleness.

Maybe you find yourself in a different category than what I have listed. Paul sums it all up in this verse, *"But to the rest speak I..."* If you find yourself with a different shape of scar than everyone else, then take this time to reflect upon that and give that situation to the Lord.

Remember, even after your sins are forgiven, the scars are still there. Even after the wound is healed, the scar is still visible. Scars show that you are battle tested. They show that you have been through tough times and rough places, but that you have healed.

II Corinthians 7:8-10 says,

"For though I made you sorry with a letter, I do not repent, though I did repent: for I perceive that the same epistle hath made you sorry, though it were but for a season. Now I rejoice, not that ye were made sorry, but that ye sorrowed to repentance: for ye were made sorry after a godly manner, that ye might receive damage by us in nothing. For godly sorrow worketh repentance to salvation not to be repented of: but the sorrow of the world worketh death."

Sorrow is always a result of sin, but sometimes we feel sorry because someone confronts our sin. More confrontation of sin is needed today! Paul made some of the Corinthians sorry by writing to them in his first epistle and calling out their sexual sin. Paul rejoiced that his obedience to the Lord allowed them to be sorry back to repentance unto God. Godly sorrow works repentance in our life!

Never allow the scars of sin to keep you from living for Christ. Give Him your wounds and allow Him to heal them. Let your scars push you forward and not leave you behind. We need more parents, family members, friends, preachers and church members who will stand up against sin for the benefit of the sinner.

II Corinthians 2:7 says, *"So that contrariwise ye ought rather to forgive him, and comfort him, lest perhaps such a one should be swallowed up with overmuch sorrow."* Do not allow any person to be swallowed up in their sorrow. We are called to comfort one another and build each other up for the glory of God.

II Corinthians 2:4 says, *"For out of much affliction and anguish of heart I wrote unto you with many tears; not that ye should be grieved, but that ye might know the love which I have more abundantly unto you."* Paul realized that sin must be dealt with, but it must be dealt with in love. You can never show a person they have a problem and not offer them a solution. What if we all had a love for the bruised, a love for the backslidden, and a love for the brethren!

Regardless of the shape of your scars, you cannot move on to "seeking singleness" if you have not given your whole heart to God. Please examine your life and give an earnest prayer to God before you move any further in this book.

Chapter 4:
Solitude in Singleness

Did you know that there is a difference between the word solitude and loneliness? People typically use these words synonymously and see no difference in the meaning of them. They both deal with being alone, but there is one word that distinguishes them. Solitude is simply being alone; whereas, loneliness is the <u>sadness</u> that results from being alone. There will always be loneliness in your single life, unless you find solitude in singleness. Let us examine the lives of two different people to better understand this truth.

David's Loneliness

If we return to the record of David and Bathsheba's sin in II Samuel chapter eleven, we can clearly see that loneliness leads to sin.

> *"And it came to pass, after the year was expired, at the time when kings go forth to battle, that David sent Joab, and his servants with him, and all Israel; and they destroyed the children of Ammon, and besieged Rabbah. But David tarried still at Jerusalem. And it came to pass in an eveningtide, that David arose from off his bed, and walked upon the roof of the king's house: and from the roof he saw a woman washing herself; and the woman was very beautiful to look upon."*

Let's pay attention to a few key words and phrases that can better help us understand David's loneliness.

The first expression, *"at the time when kings go forth to battle,"* infers this was a designed time when the king had a duty to uphold. This was a time he had to mentally, physically, and spiritually prepare for the battle that was up ahead. David should have been going forth to battle; however, he sent Joab in his place. The next sentence says, *"but David <u>tarried</u> still at Jerusalem."*

When he was out of the way of his <u>duty</u>, he was in the way of the <u>devil</u>. When he <u>tarried</u>, he was <u>tempted</u>.

The next verse says, *"David arose from off his bed."* David was already in a vulnerable state by not upholding the duty the Lord had given him; now, he is being idle. Idleness in the Christian walk gives great advantage to the tempter. David began by simply spending time in solitude. However, his solitude provoked him to idleness. As his idleness began to build on his bed, it led him to loneliness. Once he reached loneliness, he walked upon the roof and was looking for anything to fill his sadness. This is the moment that he had let his guard down and sin had first entered his heart. We can connect loneliness directly to sin. Most of the time, your loneliness leads you to temptation and submission of sin.

If David would have been doing his duty for the Lord, he could have escaped this whole problem. How does this apply to our lives? I believe it encourages us to never get to the point in our walk with Christ that we let our guard down. The easiest time to do this is when you are idle. David's idleness not only caused him to <u>look</u> upon things that he ought not, but to <u>do</u> things that he ought not. Never allow yourself to be idle in the Lord's work. Continue where God has called you to be and never drop your duty!

Christ's Solitude

Let us now turn our attention to the life of Jesus Christ to see how we can seek solitude in singleness. Matthew 4:1 says, *"Then was Jesus led up of the Spirit into the wilderness to be tempted of the devil."* If Jesus Christ was tempted by the tempter, then so will we. Notice that the Spirit led Him to the <u>wilderness</u> to be tempted. The Spirit led Him to a place of <u>solitude</u> before he was allowed to be tempted. Christ, unlike David, would not allow His solitude to turn into idleness. The account ends with, *"Then saith Jesus unto him, Get thee hence, Satan: for it is written, Thou shalt worship the Lord thy God, and him only shalt thou serve. Then the devil leaveth him, and behold, angels came and ministered unto him."*

Besides the obvious answer that Jesus Christ was God in human flesh, how do you think He was able to withstand the

—

temptations of the tempter? By prayer. Jesus surrounded his life with prayer. When he was not preaching, teaching, and discipling, he was praying. Praying was what kept his solitude from turning into idleness, and so should it be for you. Let's look at a few examples:

Jesus prayed in the morning. Mark 1:35 says, *"And in the morning, rising up a great while before day, he went out, and departed into a solitary place, and there prayed."* I have always struggled with waking up early, but look at the emphasis that is placed on the time of prayer. Jesus arose before the sun arose to pray for the mission work of that day. May we learn to value the importance of morning prayer as Christ.

Jesus prayed through the night. Luke 6:12-13 says, *"And it came to pass in those days, that he went out into a mountain to pray, and continued all night in prayer to God. And when it was day, he called unto him his disciples: and of them he chose twelve, whom also he named apostles."* Not only did Christ pray in the morning before the sun arose, but he also prayed after the sun had set. Jesus ended his night with prayer and occasionally prayed through the night! Why did he do this? The Bible says, *"he chose twelve"* the next day. He had a big decision coming that next day and needed to be surrendered to God in his decision making. How much better would our decisions be if we would pray through the night as Christ!

Jesus prayed when he was sorrowful. Matthew 26:36-39 says, *"Then cometh Jesus with them unto a place called Gethsemane, and saith unto the disciples, Sit ye here, while I go and pray yonder. And he took with him Peter and the two sons of Zebedee, and began to be sorrowful and very heavy. Then saith he unto them, My soul is exceeding sorrowful, even unto death: tarry ye here, and watch with me. And he went a little further, and fell on his face, and prayed."* When Jesus's soul was sorrowful, He took friends with him to pray. Not only had he surrounded his life in prayer, he surrounded his life with praying people. Notice how Jesus left the disciples and went a little further to pray alone before God. Even in the midst of others, we can seek solitude with God. May we pray when our souls are sorrowful!

Jesus prayed for power. Luke 5:16-17 says, *"And he withdrew himself into the wilderness, and prayed. And it came to pass on a certain day, as he was teaching, that there were Pharisees and doctors of the law sitting by, which were come out of every town of Galilee, and Judaea, and Jerusalem: and the power of the Lord was present to heal them."* I have always heard, "there is power in prayer!" This statement cannot be real to you until you experience that power personally. In order to experience it, you have to pray. Look at how Jesus went into the wilderness and prayed. A short time after he prayed, *"the power of the Lord was present."* Do you see the direct correlation between power and prayer? May we seek to pray for power as Christ!

Jesus prayed for people. Luke 22:31-32 says, *"And the Lord said, Simon, Simon, behold, Satan hath desired to have you, that he may sift you as wheat: But I have prayed for thee, that thy faith fail not."* Not only did Jesus pray for himself in times of temptation, but he prayed that other people would be able to overcome it too. May we have a burden to pray for people like Christ!

Jesus prayed alone. Matthew 14:22-23 says, *"And straightway Jesus constrained his disciples to get into a ship, and to go before him unto the other side, while he sent the multitudes away. And when he had sent the multitudes away, he went up into a mountain apart to pray: and when the evening was come, he was there alone."* First, Jesus sent all of the multitudes away, then he began to pray. We should value prayers with believers in church, but may we see the need for prayer alone as Christ did!

Jesus prayed in solitude. Mark 1:35 says, *"And in the morning, rising up a great while before day, he went out, and departed into a solitary place, and there prayed."* Jesus prayed in a *"solitary place,"* meaning he prayed in solitude. We should have comfort knowing that Christ was seeking solitude in His singleness with the Father. What an example He is unto us. May we pray in solitude of singleness like Christ! May we model our prayer life after Christ!

Societies Solitude

The most frightening thing in our culture is to be alone. For most people, a phone is their distraction from being left alone. The next time you are in public, look at people who are sitting alone and observe what they are doing. The majority of them will be on their phones in some sort of capacity. When silence is present, God penetrates your heart. It is in silence that God's still small voice speaks, and that is why many people do not like to spend time in solitude. Many of you claim "you do not have time," however, this usually means that you do not want to listen to what God has to say.

I remember being in high school and going through the breakup of a relationship. In all of my sorrow, do you know what the first thing I turned to was? Snapchat. Instead of <u>seeking solitude</u> in God's Word, I <u>looked toward loneliness</u> in my phone. Why? Because snapchat gave me the ability to feel as if I was not alone. I surrounded myself with many conversations and with many different people so that I would never be alone or have to face the silence. I wanted God's still small voice to speak to me, but I was not willing to sit in the silence. Isaiah 34:16 says, *"seek ye out the book of the Lord, and read."* Stop seeking out snapchat and start seeking out your study time in God's Word! Snapchat doesn't have the answers to your problems, but God's Word does!

I Thessalonians 4:11 says, *"And that ye study to be quiet, and to do your own business, and to work with your own hands, as we commanded you."* Seek solitude in singleness through study and prayer.

Take this time to answer the questions for Chapters 1-4 on the self-evaluation page of the beginning of this book.

Chapter 5:
Surety in Singleness

Surety is the state of being sure or certain of something. As we jump back to our core passage in I Corinthians chapter seven, we can be assured that it is indeed alright to be single.

Paul writes in verse six, *"But I speak this by permission, and not of commandment."* Before beginning to discuss the issue of singleness, he gives the authority upon which he speaks. God had given him permission to pen through the inspiration of the Holy Spirit. Such an issue as singleness cannot be explained from man's opinions or experiences; it must come directly from God.

He continues in verse seven, *"For I would that all men were even as I myself."* By permission of the Holy Spirit, Paul says that he wished all men could live single as he had. This does not say that he wished no man would be given in marriage. Paul desires to see people seek singleness; whether it be for a short-time or for a life-time.

The next part of verse seven says, *"But every man hath his proper gift of God, one after this manner, and another after that."* Paul deeply wishes that all men and women would be able to experience giving their attention fully to the Lord as he was able to; however, he realizes that not everyone can. Singleness is a gift from God, just as marriage is a gift from God. The only way you can live the single life is by being given the proper gift.

Let's take this time to review our definitions. Singleness means simplicity; sincerity; purity of mind or purpose; freedom from duplicity; singleness of heart. Single means unmarried; having no companion or assistant. In these few verses, Paul specifically deals with how to seek singleness as a single person. We can be assured that there is nothing wrong with not being in a relationship.

In verse eight Paul writes, *"I say therefore unto the unmarried and the widows, it is good for them if they abide even as*

I." Not only is singleness a proper gift, but it is a good gift. Paul breaks down the two types of single people: the unmarried and the widowed. He vouches that if they have the gift of remaining in their state of being single, then it is good for them to abide.

I know what you are thinking now... how in the world could being single be a good gift? As in terms of service to the Lord, it is the best gift any man can receive. As I think back to the times when I was most committed to my walk with the Lord, it was always when I was single.

Verse thirty-two describes this perfectly, *"He that is unmarried careth for the things that belong to the Lord, how he may please the Lord."* If you are single, regardless of your age or the circumstance, my challenge to you is to meditate on this verse. Use your singleness to glorify God to the utmost of your ability.

You may say, "well, I know I am single right now, but I also know that I do not have the gift of singleness." Well, I can assure you that is alright too! If you are single, you need to be seeking singleness in heart with God. I have found it to be true in my own life that when I got my relationship with the Lord right, then he began preparing me to get my relationship with a young lady right.

Verse seventeen gives us deeper insight about how to abide in our calling, *"But as God hath distributed to every man, as the Lord hath called every one, so let him walk."* We do not pick and choose our gifts. It is God who distributes them as he sees fit in our life. Do you remember how God saw the need for Adam to have a wife? Do you remember how he filled that need? God will do the same thing in your life. If he has called you to abide in singleness, then he will distribute you the gift to be able to remain in singleness. May we walk as the Lord has called us, not only in our relationship status, but in the Christian life.

Paul summarizes the thought of "the called" in verse twenty-four. *"Brethren, let every man, wherein he is called, therein abide with God."* Paul places special emphasis on a profound truth in this verse. In our own power, we will not be able to walk where God is leading. In our own ability, we will not be able to abide where God has called. But, *"with God,"* we will have the strength to walk and abide where He has called. God doesn't call those who are already equipped; He equips those whom he has called. No matter what God calls us to do, we can be assured that He will be with us every step of the way. Where God guides, He provides.

If you are single, my advice to you is based on the Word of God: pray that God would see your need and meet your need. Ask God for assurance and peace in the midst of your singleness.

Whether you are fifteen years old and are looking for a boyfriend or girlfriend. Whether you are twenty-six years old looking for your life mate. Or whether you are sixty years old and are a widow or widower seeking direction from God. Ask God to allow you to see the importance of singleness.

The best advice that I can give you through my experience is to wait on the Lord. Psalm 27:14 says, *"Wait on the LORD: be of good courage, and he shall strengthen thine heart: wait, I say, on the LORD."*

Instead of looking for a relationship, begin seeking singleness. The moment you begin to seek the Lord with all of your heart is the moment that God will begin to reveal your needs that must be filled. There is surety in singleness!

Chapter 6:
Sincerity in Singleness

Paul would not have sought to give us surety of singleness if there was no sincerity in singleness. Singleness to God is a sincere matter. Since it is a sincere matter to God, it should be a sincere matter to us. Paul took on the burden of the Lord for singleness, but can we do the same?

The Sincerity of our Sentiment

The basis of our study of singleness has come from Paul's epistle to the church at Corinth. We know that Paul was sentimental to the state of singleness in the lives of new believers. In I Corinthians 7:35, Paul expressed, *"And this I speak for your own profit; not that I may cast a snare upon you, but for that which is comely, and that ye may attend upon the Lord without distraction."* Paul assures the people of Corinth that these letters are for their own profit. He wanted Corinth to realize their sin, repent of their sin, and rebuke their sin. Paul had no profit to gain; it was all for the people's profit.

Paul emphasized that he did not write to cast a snare upon them. He is not one of the false teachers who are trying to lead the flock of God astray. He wrote with one goal, to see them attend upon the Lord without distraction. This is why he goes so in debt about sexual sin within the city and the church. Much <u>distraction</u> began to cause <u>inaction</u>.

The heart that Paul had for the Lord's work is best seen in II Corinthians 2:4, *"For out of much affliction and anguish of heart I wrote unto you with many tears; not that ye should be grieved, but that ye might know the love which I have more abundantly unto you."* If the issue of singleness to God was not sincere, then a grown man like Paul would not have been shedding tears over it. Paul's goal was not to see the people grieved from the sorrow of sin, but to see them given the love of Christ. We must not resent seeking sincere sentiment!

41

The Sincerity of our Simplicity

II Corinthians 1:12 says, *"For our rejoicing is this, the testimony of our conscience, that in simplicity and godly sincerity, not with fleshly wisdom, but by the grace of God, we have had our conversation in the world, and more abundantly to you-ward."* Paul rejoices that the gospel is simple. He proclaims the sincerity of the simplicity of the gospel. Godly sincerity is not found in fleshly wisdom. Neither can the simplicity of the gospel be revealed in fleshly wisdom. Both simplicity and sincerity are only possible through the grace of God.

Paul had preached this message to all the world, but more abundantly to the church of Corinth. II Corinthians 11:3 says, *"But I fear, lest by any means, as the serpent beguiled Eve through his subtilty, so your minds should be corrupted from the simplicity that is in Christ."* While the gospel is composed of simplicity, Satan attempts to corrupt by subtilty. Paul's fear was that the people of Corinth would overthink the simplicity of Christ and fall into the snare of Satan. Paul did not write to Corinth to *"cast a snare,"* but Satan is the subtle creature who would.

I Corinthians 2:14 says, *"But the natural man receiveth not the things of the Spirit of God: for they are foolishness unto him: neither can he know them, because they are spiritually discerned."* Have you ever wondered why some of the smartest scientists in the world cannot understand the simplicity of the gospel? It's because they are trying to scientifically discern the Bible and not spiritually discern it. To be spiritual, we must be scriptural. Likewise, to be scriptural, we must be spiritual.

The Sincerity of our Sanctity

I Thessalonians 3:13 says, *"To the end he may stablish your hearts unblameable in holiness before God…"* The word holiness can also be translated as "sanctification." Here it refers to the consecration of the believer to God in holy and proper behavior in regard to sexual purity. The goal of Paul's confrontation of the sexual sin in Thessalonica was to see the people's hearts stablished

---

in holiness before God. God still seeks for believers to have holy hearts before Him.

Building upon holiness, I Peter 1:15-16 says, *"But as he which hath called you is holy, so be ye holy in all manner of conversation; Because it is written, Be ye holy; for I am holy."* God is holy, and, as His children, we are instructed to be holy. God does not say that we are to only be holy in deeds, church attendance, or tithing. He says to be holy *"in all manner of conversation,"* meaning that everything we think, say, or do should be hovered with holiness.

The Sincerity of our Separation

The call to holiness brings the command for separation. I Thessalonians 4:3-4 says, *"For this is the will of God, even your sanctification, that ye should abstain from fornication: That every one of you should know how to possess his vessel in sanctification and honor."* The will of God is for us to be made holy so that we can abstain from sin. In this case, the sin was specified as the sexual sin of fornication. Fornication is sexual sin that deviates from God's standard. The word fornication, as used in this verse, would include premarital sex, incest, homosexuality, bestiality, and adultery. In a world that is burning for such sin, God's standard for separation still remains the same.

I Thessalonians 5:22-23 says, *"Abstain from all appearance of evil. And the very God of peace sanctify you wholly; and I pray God your whole spirit and soul and body be preserved blameless unto the coming of our Lord Jesus Christ."* To sanctify something would mean to separate, set apart, or to make holy. God expects us to abstain from the very things which may have even the smallest form of evil.

What does it mean for God to sanctify us wholly? He will make us wholly holy. It sounds funny, right? God will make us complete through our life of holiness. Holiness is not just defined by your spirit; however, Paul asserts that it is defined in your spirit, soul and body. We cannot give only one part of our body to holiness. When we give our life to Christ, we must give Him our all! We are not to remain holy only for a few days, weeks, or years. We are to remain holy and *"be preserved blameless unto the coming of our Lord Jesus Christ."* When you give your life to Christ, make sure to give it for a life-time, not a short-time!

Your sincerity should be marked by your separation to God and from the world. You cannot live for God if you have not separated from the world.

The Sincerity of our Single State

We must conclude this chapter with the sincerity of singleness while you are single. I Corinthians 7:32-33, *"But I would have you without carefulness. He that is unmarried careth for the things that belong to the Lord, how he may please the Lord: But he that is married careth for the things that are of the world, how he may please his wife."* Serving the Lord is a serious matter. There is no better time to get serious about serving Him than when you are single. Did you know that even when you are single, you are still working to build a relationship? Not a relationship with a man or woman, but a relationship with God. Being sincere in your relationship with God while you are single can produce two major factors in your life: self-love and selflessness.

Selflessness will be discussed in detail under the chapter "Sacrifice in Singleness." Selflessness means to let go of self; the opposite of selfishness. Ironically, when we are single, we must seek to let go of self and give all to God.

Even more ironic is that self-love will be the result of your selflessness. The worldly definition of self-love is "the love of self." It is further defined as "an appreciation of one's own worth or virtue; proper regard for an attention to one's own happiness or well-being." The world's definition of self-love is very selfish. Scripturally, we find self-love by living up to the Lord's love. You will find happiness through your holiness.

In Matthew 22:36, the Pharisees sought to tempt Jesus by saying, *"Master, which is the great commandment in the law?"* Verse thirty-seven and thirty-eight records Christ's profound answer; *"Jesus said unto him, Thou shalt love the Lord thy God with all thy heart, and with all thy soul, and with all thy mind. This is the first and great commandment."* They were all shocked because Jesus's answer was not one of the ten commandments written on stone. While His answer may not have been a <u>recorded</u> commandment, it was the <u>root</u> of all the commandments. Before you can experience self-love, you must experience the Savior's love. You must love the Lord with your entire being; your spirit, soul, body, heart, and mind.

Jesus continued in verse thirty-nine, *"And the second is like unto it, Thou shalt love thy neighbor as thyself."* The second commandment is the <u>result</u> of the <u>root</u> of the first commandment. The <u>root</u> is love for God; the <u>result</u> is love for man. Self-love isn't about the <u>happiness</u> of yourself, it's about your <u>holiness</u> to God. Self-love is not about the care of yourself, it's about your contentment in Christ. You will never learn to love yourself, if you do not learn to love the Lord. Likewise, you will never be able to learn to love someone else, if you do not first love yourself. Spend your singleness learning to love God and finding your self-love in Him.

We all need a dose of that selfless, self-love that comes from the Savior! This is the sincerity of Singleness.

Take this time to answer the questions for Chapters 5-6 on the self-evaluation page of the beginning of this book.

Chapter 7:
Surrendering in Singleness

The word "surrender" is never found in the Bible; however, the principle of surrendering is present. Surrender is the action of yielding one's person or giving up the power of another. We have heard "surrender to Christ as your personal savior" for all of our lives. But what does it really mean to surrender? It means to yield your life completely to Christ. You are not only giving up your person, but also your possessions. The goal of surrendering to the Savior, is to glorify the Savior.

Surrendering to the Savior

Proverbs 3:5-6 has been my life verse over the last year. It says, *"Trust in the Lord with all thine heart; and lean not unto thine own understanding. In all thy ways acknowledge him, and he shall direct thy paths."* In order to surrender and align your will with God's will, you must first *"trust in the Lord with all thine heart."* Notice how the word heart is emphasized here. Trusting the Lord is giving him, not just part of, but ALL of your heart.

The hardest thing to do is the next part of the verse, *"and lean not unto thine own understanding."* How many days do we try to overthink God? How many times do we try to plan, organize, and coordinate our lives based on our own understanding? The Bible instructs us to <u>stop thinking</u> and <u>start trusting</u>.

The first part of verse six says, *"in all thy ways acknowledge him."* Acknowledging God doesn't mean that you simply say "thank you God." I believe many people use God as a pocket pal. They trust in their own understanding and they choose the path of life that they want to go down. Whenever a bump comes across their path, they pull God out of their pocket and begin to acknowledge Him again. Acknowledging God means to give Him the honor and glory in every path of your life. It means to put Him at His proper place, which should be at the forefront of your life.

———

The last part of verse six says, *"and he shall direct thy paths."* If you would stop thinking, start trusting, and stay acknowledging, then God will direct the paths of your life. On the flip side, God will not direct your paths until you take these three steps.

Take it from my personal experience over the last year. At the beginning of 2021, I started reading this verse and I began to pray that God would direct my paths in three different areas; in a Relationship, Career, and the Ministry. After praying for months, I felt like God was not answering my prayer nor directing my paths. At this point, the natural man stepped in and said "you know what God? If you won't direct my paths, then I will start making my own." I immediately began to force my own relationship, my own career, and my own direction in the ministry.

After about six months, I had reached the point where I was ready to give up on everything that I had worked so hard for. Why? Because I was not operating in the power and the blessing of the Lord. I had not allowed Him to direct my paths. I took over the Lord's position in my life. What is most ironic about this is after I got a girlfriend, a job, and an offer to pastor a local church, I acknowledged God. I told everyone "well, God has blessed me with a relationship, a job, and direction in the ministry," however I had directed myself.

Do you want to know what the outcome of these things were? They all failed. My relationship was not the relationship I needed to be in. That relationship had to be ended. My job was not the career I needed to be in. That job had to be resigned. The place in the ministry was not the place I needed to be in. That opportunity had to be turned down. There was nothing wrong with the girl, job, or church… they were just not God's paths!

After much prayer, the Lord gave me Proverbs 3:5-6 again. This time when I read it, it meant a little bit more to me than the first. I began to take God seriously. I began to seek singleness in my heart with God. I began to trust in him fully. I began to lean on Him, rather than my own understanding. I began to acknowledge Him in every part of my life. Do you know what happened next? He began to direct my paths, just as His Word promised.

Surrendering in your State

Our flesh seeks fleshly desires. Philippians 2:21 says, *"For all seek their own, not the things which are Jesus Christ's."* The natural man seeks his own destination and he chooses his own path of getting there. Many times, you are so stuck on our will, that you forget to surrender to God's will.

The unmarried man seeks the things of Jesus Christ. I Corinthians 7:32 says, *"He that is unmarried careth for the things that belong to the Lord, how he may please the Lord."* The single man who has surrendered his heart to the Lord is not seeking for his own pleasure, he is seeking to please the Lord.

The unmarried woman seeks the things of Jesus Christ. I Corinthians 7:34 says, *"There is a difference also between a wife and a virgin. The unmarried woman careth for the things of the Lord, that she may be holy both in body and in spirit."* The single woman who has surrendered her heart to the Lord is not seeking for her own <u>happiness</u>, she is seeking <u>holiness</u> before the Lord.

The widow seeks the things of Jesus Christ. I Timothy 5:5 says, *"Now she that is a widow indeed, and desolate, trusteth in God, and continueth in supplications and prayers night and day."* The widow that has surrendered her heart to the Lord, trusts in God and continues in prayers at all times. Whenever her state of singleness begins to bring sorrow, she prays. Whenever the scars of singleness begin to resurface, she prays. Whenever the solitude of singleness begins to turn into loneliness, she prays. Her life is marked by prayer, and through prayer she gains the surety of singleness.

Not only must surrendering be marked by prayer, but it must be marked by selflessness. How ironic does that sound? Selflessness in the midst of your singleness. Most people begin to think selfishly when they are single. "Everything is about me and it is all mine." However, everything should be about Him and be all His!

Above are true examples of people "seeking singleness" while they are single. Whether you are single or not, my question to you is, have you surrendered to the will of God in your life? Don't force God into the center of your will, put yourself into the center of His will. Surrender to the <u>Word of God</u>, the <u>Work of God</u>, and the <u>Will of God</u>. You cannot seek singleness until you learn to surrender to the Savior!

Surrendering as a Student: To the Bible College Student

"The LORD is good unto them that wait for him, to the soul that seeketh him" (Lamentations 3:25).

Who led you to Bible College? I hope your answer would be "the Lord," but it may not be. Maybe you came to Bible College because your parents forced you to. Maybe you came because your pastor pushed you to. Maybe you came because your friend wanted you to. Maybe you came because your girlfriend or boyfriend begged you to.

What made you want to come to Bible College? I hope your answer would be to study and prepare yourself for the ministry, but it may not be. Maybe you came because it was your only option. Maybe you came because it was a cheaper alternative. Maybe you came because you couldn't decide what else to do. Maybe you came because you were looking for "the one."

I made so many excuses of why I shouldn't go to Bible College. I used my job, my relationship, and my current position in ministry as excuses to make my own plan in the midst of God's path. I used my little cousin as an excuse; he needed a good Christian influence. I used my grandpa as an excuse; he's getting older and I need to spend as much time with him as I can. I used my job as an excuse; I need to have a regular source of income so I can keep tithing and supporting the church. I used my church as an excuse; I have to be involved because the people are limited and they need me. Notice the most common word in all of my excuses; "I". It was never about everyone else, it was about me not wanting to sacrifice, surrender and serve where I knew I needed to.

Isaiah 55:8-9 says, *"For my thoughts are not your thoughts, neither are your ways my ways, saith the LORD. For as the heavens are higher than the earth, so are my ways higher than your ways, and my thoughts than your thoughts."* Whatever your excuses are, stop making them.

Why did I come to Crown College of the Bible? I came to seek singleness. I left a lot behind to come and gain this experience. Do not take your time for granted while you are here. Maybe you did come for the wrong reason, but don't let that hold you back from where you are now. You are here to prepare your heart for the ministry, regardless if that was your initial reason or not. You are here to serve the Lord. You are here to grow in your relationship with God. You are here, so you must begin "Seeking Singleness."

Before coming on campus, I had a conversation with a young lady about the life of a single student at Bible College. The feedback she gave me was as follows:

"I think specifically a lot of girls struggle with it, because you see other girls finding people and moving along and it's really hard to be happy for them. I really struggled for a while with that, but I'm working on my contentment with the stage I'm at in life. More specifically, in Christian colleges there can be a lot of pressure for relationships and finding the one."

"Honestly though, during this time [of singleness] my relationship with the Lord has grown and my faith has become so much more real to me. I've become bolder and more comfortable talking about Him and find myself bringing Him up all the time."

"My theme this past semester was to 'wait on the Lord.' And boy, patience has been tried. My mom keeps telling me, 'you asked for patience, He's trying to help you.'"

I understood with my mind what this young lady said, but I could not connect with it in my heart. Now that I have been to Bible College, I can assure every part of what she said to be true. Bible College shouldn't be the place to find your mate, it should be the place to grow in grace. The pressures of relationships are real. The sorrow of singleness is sincere.

Many of you young ladies and gentlemen are so busy <u>looking</u> that you aren't <u>learning</u>. You are so focused on finding your life's mate, that you haven't taken time to be satisfied in your state. You find a boyfriend or girlfriend you did not pray about, and then you acknowledge God for blessing you with them. Was it really the <u>Lord's blessing</u> or was it <u>Satan's beguiling</u>? God has great plans for you while you are here; don't be confused between blessing and beguiling. In the words of that young lady, "wait on the Lord."

When you get so fixed on looking for a mate, you forsake to look at yourself. Many times, you want from someone else what you are not willing to give:

> Young man, you want a godly wife, but you don't want to sacrifice to live a godly life.

> Young lady, you want a godly man, but you don't want to surrender to live in God's plan.

Being single is not a sin! Take time in your singleness, especially at Bible College, to grow in your relationship with God. Remember, *"Trust in the LORD with all thine heart; and lean not unto thine own understanding. In all thy ways acknowledge him, and he shall direct thy paths."* The Lord will direct your path. If God is waiting to reveal the path, then believe that he will give you peace to trust the process.

"The LORD is good unto them that wait for him, to the soul that seeketh him." Surrender your soul. Seek singleness. Wait for Him.

Chapter 8:
Servanthood in Singleness

A crucial part of seeking singleness is surrendering to serve. We must be careful not to confuse a servant with a slave. While both words are correlative in their entitlement to a master, they have very different meanings. A servant's subjection to his master is <u>voluntary</u>, whereas the slave's is <u>mandatory</u>. I believe that we can observe the record of David, the sacrifice of Christ, and the teachings of Paul to conclude what true "servanthood in singleness" is.

Characteristics of a Servant

There are several things that come to mind when the name David is mentioned. Some would immediately think of the story of David and Goliath. Others would go straight to the story of David and Bathsheba. What ought to be our first conception however, is the state of his heart.

We find two places in the Word of God where David's heart is characterized by God:

> *"But now the kingdom shall not continue: the LORD hath sought him <u>a man after his own heart</u>, and the LORD hath commanded him to be captain over his people, because thou hast not kept that which the LORD commanded thee"* (I Samuel 13:14).

> *"And when he had removed him, he raised up unto them David to be their king; to whom also he gave testimony, and said, I have found David the son of Jesse, <u>a man after mine own heart</u>, which shall fulfil all my will"* (Acts 13:22).

Is it possible for us to have a heart after God's own heart? Let's examine the life of David to better understand how he received this title from God.

II Samuel 3:18 says, *"Now then do it: for the LORD hath spoken of David, saying, By the hand of <u>my servant</u> David I will save my people Israel out of the hand of the Philistines, and out of the hand of all their enemies."* Not only did God refer to David as a man after His own heart, but He calls him his servant. There is a direct connection between a servant and his heart. I believe that in order to be a <u>servant of God</u>, you will have to have the right <u>heart for God</u>. The heart has been emphasized in every chapter up to this point, and it will not end here.

In the description of David as a servant, I believe we find four main characteristics of a heart for God:

The first characteristic of a servant is <u>the knowledge of his heart</u>. II Samuel 7:20-21 says, *"And what can David say more unto thee? For thou, Lord GOD, knowest thy servant. For thy word's sake, and according to thine own heart, hast thou done all these great things, to make thy servant know them."* To begin, David acknowledges that he is the servant of God. The first step in becoming a true servant for Christ is to know and acknowledge that you are one. After we have acknowledged our servanthood, we must then learn our master's heart. God did great and mighty things in the life of David so that he could learn His heart. How are you going to model your heart after God's if you cannot see God's heart? Thankfully, God has given us <u>His Word</u> and <u>His Wonders</u> so that His servants can know His heart.

The second characteristic of a servant is <u>the obedience of his heart</u>. II Samuel 7:27 says, *"For thou, O LORD of hosts, God of Israel, hast revealed to thy servant, saying, I will build thee an house: therefore hath thy servant found in his heart to pray this prayer unto thee."* God had to first reveal His heart before David could follow His heart. We learned in the previous chapter that God revealed Himself through His Word and wonders. God's method of revealing Himself to His servants has not changed. Once God had revealed his heart, David saw the need to be connected with His heart. How can we be connected to the heart of God? David gives us the simple answer: prayer. When God begins to reveal Himself unto you, the best thing you can do is to get down on your knees and pray. Align your heart with God's heart through the power of prayer!

The third characteristic of a servant is <u>the repentance of his heart</u>. II Samuel 24:10 says, *"And David's heart smote him after he had numbered the people. And David said unto the LORD, I have sinned greatly in that I have done: and now, I beseech thee, O LORD, take away the iniquity of thy servant; for I have done very foolishly."* Notice what it was that smote David; his heart. While the heart is the root where sin begins, it is also the root where repentance begins. The Lord began to do the work of <u>revealing</u>, but David had to do the work of <u>repenting</u>. Once David was <u>convicted</u> of his sin, he <u>confessed</u> his sin.

Many people <u>regret</u> their sin, but do not truly <u>repent</u> of it. May I say that regret is not enough to be a servant of God, you must be repentant from the heart. What is the difference between repentance and regret? Regret is associated with shame and embarrassment of your sin. Repentance is associated with acknowledging your sin. <u>Regret</u> leads to <u>retreat</u>, but <u>repentance</u> leads to a <u>right heart</u> with God.

The fourth characteristic of a servant is <u>the mediation of his heart</u>. Psalms 119:23 says, "But thy servant did meditate in thy statutes." I believe many Christians have misplaced memorization with meditation. Do you know that in the Bible, the word "memorization" is never mentioned once? While the principle of memorizing God's Word is found, the word itself never is. Many of us are so busy trying to memorize God's Word with our mind, that we forget to meditate on God's Word in our hearts. Memorization <u>of</u> God's Word is the result of Meditation <u>in</u> God's Word.

Christ-likeness of a Servant

What better place is there to look at the characteristics of a true servant than to Jesus Christ himself? Philippians 2:5-8 says,

> *"Let this mind be in you, which was also in Christ Jesus: Who being in the form of God, thought it not robbery to be equal with God: But made himself of no reputation, and took upon him the form of a servant, and was made in the likeness of men: And being found in fashion as a man, he humbled*

55

himself, and became obedient unto death, even the death of the cross."

Read these words again, *"and took upon him the form of a servant."* Christ was made a servant for our sake! Notice the characteristics of Christ's servant heart. First, he was humble. Second, he was obedient. Third, he was surrendered. The King of Kings and the Lord of Lords humbled himself to be a servant. The One who didn't have to die, came and was obedient unto the Father all the way to death. The same Christ that we must surrender to serve, willingly surrendered His life on the cross of Calvary.

Calling of a Servant

Now we must observe the teachings of Paul from our core passage. I Corinthians 7:22-23 says, *"For he that is called in the Lord, being a servant, is the Lord's freeman: likewise also he that is called, being free, is Christ's servant. Ye are bought with a price; be not ye the servants of men."* A freeman is a man who has power over himself. He can do whatever he wants to do, at whatever time he wants to do it. No one is in control of what he chooses to do. The scripture above describes a man who was once the servant of another master. However, when he was called by the Lord, he became a freeman. The Lord has set him free from his bondage. Who the Lord has set him free, is now Christ's servant.

As Christians, having received and accepted the call to God, we are made servants of God. We have been given freedom and liberty in Christ Jesus! Paul continues in verse twenty-three by emphasizing the value of our freedom. Our freedom was bought with a price… a very valuable price. We were bought by the sacrifice of our Savior. Since this was such a valuable <u>price</u>, Paul encourages believers to cherish and live up to the <u>possession</u>.

Let's say that you have been saving up to buy a brand-new Chevrolet Silverado that costs $45,000. You work for three years and finally, through all the blood, sweat and tears, you have saved enough money to pay cash for your new truck. You are going to cherish this truck because you put valuable time, effort and work into it. You are going to make sure that it stays washed, waxed, and

---

56

looking sharp. You are going to keep it maintained because you want this truck to last for your life-time. You don't put anything on it but the highest quality products, and you don't put anything in it that is not the best of the best.

Now, if we will cherish the cost of a vehicle that way, how much more should we cherish the cost of our freedom in Christ? The best part is, we didn't have to pay anything for it! Maybe this is why so many Christians don't value their possession. When we do not have to pay a price for our possession, we often overlook it. Do not go back to being a servant of sin if you have been bought to be a servant to men. That is using low-quality products on a high-quality purchase!

Romans 6:16-18 says,

"Know ye not, that to whom ye yield yourselves servants to obey, his servants ye are to whom ye obey; whether of sin unto death, or of obedience unto righteousness? But God be thanked, that ye were the servants of sin, but ye have obeyed from the heart that form of doctrine which was delivered you. Being then made free from sin, ye became the servants of righteousness."

No longer are we slaves of sin, but servants of Him! If you obey sin, then you are the slave of sin and it is your master. If you obey and follow Christ, then you are the servant of the Savior and He is your Master. Every slave is a servant, but every servant is not a slave! The words, *"whether of sin unto death,"* remind me of Romans 6:23, *"For the wages of sin is death; but the gift of God is eternal life through Jesus Christ our Lord."* Serving sin is going to take you to death, hell, and eternal separation from God. Serving the Savior is going to take you to life, heaven, and eternal separation from Satan.

Notice how the verse states that they *"obeyed from the heart."* Throughout this book, our main issues are the things of the heart. We must believe by the heart, obey by the heart, and serve by the heart!

57

Paul continues in Galatians 1:10, *"For do I now persuade men, or God? Or do I seek to please men? For if I yet pleased men, I should not be the servant of Christ."* If we seek to please ourselves, then we are not true servants. If we seek to please others, then we are not true servants. To be a servant of Christ, we must forfeit all desires of the flesh and align our hearts with the desires of God.

Paul expounds upon this idea in Colossians 3:23-24, *"And whatsoever ye do, do it heartily, as to the Lord, and not unto men; Knowing that of the Lord ye shall receive the reward of the inheritance: for ye serve the Lord Christ."* We are taking the work of the Lord <u>to men</u>, but we are doing the work of the Lord <u>for Him</u>.

In Ephesians 6:5 Paul commands, *"Servants, be obedient to them that are your masters according to the flesh, with fear and trembling, in singleness of your heart, as unto Christ;"* It pleases the Lord when we follow his commandments. The first commandment is to be obedient. If there is anything that defines a servant, it is his obedience. This verse is calling for obedience to earthly masters, whether that be to princes, positions, presidents or parents. The bottom line is that we must be obedient unto our earthly masters in singleness of our hearts, as we are unto Christ. You cannot be a servant of the Savior unless you are seeking singleness of heart.

Paul proclaimed in I Corinthians 9:19, *"For though I be free from all men, yet have I made myself servant unto all, that I might gain the more."* While we do not seek to <u>please</u> men, we must seek to <u>serve</u> them. If we love God, then we will love His Word. If we love His Word, then we will love His people. Being servants <u>of</u> Christ will make us servants <u>to</u> the world. God did not create puppets; He created people. He gave us the right to choose to be made a true servant of Christ.

II Corinthians 4:5 says, *"For we preach not ourselves, but Christ Jesus the Lord; and ourselves your servants for Jesus' sake."* Do you remember how Christ made himself a servant? Paul was able to model his servanthood after Christ. Our goal should always be to model our lives after Him. If Christ was made a servant for our sake, then we must be made a servant for His sake.

Remember, a servant's submission is <u>voluntary</u>, but a slave's submission is <u>mandatory</u>. We should use our liberty in Christ Jesus to serve other men. With <u>liberty</u> comes much <u>responsibility</u>. With much <u>responsibility</u> comes personal <u>accountability</u>. Galatians 5:13 says, *"For, brethren, ye have been called unto liberty; only use not liberty for an occasion to the flesh, but by love serve one another."* We must serve others, with love, by our liberty.

Your servanthood will be marked by your servant heart! Seeking Singleness means we must surrender to serve.

Chapter 9:
Sacrifice in Singleness

The greatest sacrifice in singleness is the sacrifice of self. After dealing directly with the issue of sexual sin, Paul dives right into the issue of sacrifice. Do you remember how the beginning started? *"Now concerning the things whereof ye wrote unto me"* (I Corinthians 7:1). Sexual sin was not the only questionable issue that had risen in Corinth. Chapter eight verse one says, *"Now as touching things offered unto idols…"* Paul's next great task was to handle the situation of sacrifice unto idols.

Self-limitation in Sacrifice

The remainder of verse one through verse three says, *"Knowledge puffeth up, but charity edifieth. And if any man think that he knoweth any thing, he knoweth nothing yet as he ought to know. But if any man love God, the same is known of him."* Before handling the issue that was present, he begins to speak of the inward man. Notice how the biological makeup of man is centered around the heart and the mind. While there are millions of processes which must take place in between those two organs, without the brain or the heart we could not live.

Knowledge refers to the mind, whereas charity refers to the heart. *"Knowledge puffeth up"* implies a person who is made arrogant because of the amount of knowledge they retain in their mind. *"Charity edifieth"* implies a person who is being built up because of the love that they contain in their heart.

Verse two does not mean that knowledge is bad or that we shouldn't work to obtain as much as we can get. It condemns the arrogance that often follows those who have much knowledge. *"And if any man think that he knoweth any thing, he knoweth nothing yet as he ought to know."* When it comes to God and His Word, we can never know enough. Many people think they have it figured out because they have been serving in the ministry for fifty years. Others think they have it figured out because they were raised in a Baptist

Church, surrounded by solid doctrine since birth. The rest think that they have it figured out because they read their Bible in its entirety last year. You should never stop learning and growing in the Word.

II Peter 3:18 says, *"But grow in grace, and in the knowledge of our Lord and Savior Jesus Christ. To him be glory both now and for ever. Amen."* Remember in the story of David how he became idle in his duties as king? He thought he had it all figured out because he had served as king for so many years. He thought that he had it all figured out because he had been in the kingdom much of his life and learned from other kings. He thought that he had it figured out because he had fought the same battles last year. However, as soon as he let his guard down, he began to fall. Never let your guard down in the Christian walk. Grow in grace and knowledge every day that you can. Don't become too confident, but don't become too content.

After condemning the arrogance of knowledge, he condones the love of heart. Verse three says, *"but if any man love God, the same is known of him."* It is not by our knowledge that we are approved by God, but by our love for God we are *"known of him."* Again, God turns the attention right back to the condition of man's heart. In order to sacrifice in singleness, you have to stop figuring with your mind and start faithing with your heart.

I Corinthians 8:4 says, *"As concerning therefore the eating of those things that are offered in sacrifice unto idols, we know that an idol is nothing in the world, and that there is none other God but one."* Paul now directs his attention to the situation; the eating of foods offered in sacrifice to idols. The people of Corinth were basically writing to Paul and asking "Paul, is this sin?"

Let me say here, if you ever have to question whether something is sin or not, then it probably is. Even if it may not seem to be sin, it is best to abstain from it. Many people struggle with questions about smoking, drinking, masturbating, and working on the Lord's day. They wander hopelessly, never seeming to find an answer. If you are asking God whether something is sin, this usually means that He has already begun working on your heart and convicting you of that thing.

Compared to God, Paul says that idols are nothing. There is only one true God, and we know Him personally if we are saved. Even though idols are nothing, we still should not show them any attention. Our hearts and minds should be so focused and filled with the Lord that we don't have room to consider serving other idols. Idols are not only gods. Idols are anything that you put before God. This could be your girlfriend, boyfriend, phone, hobbies, sin, self, or anything else.

Technically, the Corinthians had the right to eat the same food that was offered to idols as long as they did not worship those idols. Paul does not stop expounding upon the thought there. Verses five and six continue, *"For though there be that are called gods, whether in heaven or in earth, (as there be gods many, and lords many,) But to us there is but one God, the Father, of whom are all things, and we in him; and one Lord Jesus Christ, by whom are all things, and we by him."* These may be two of the more profound doctrinal verses in all of Corinthians. To the Christian, there is only one God, the Father, who made all things. Making all things means that he also made you. As believers we are not just part of His creation, we are His children. *"We are in him,"* meaning that we have salvation, hope, faith, and a relationship with Him.

Paul doesn't stop with God the Father; he continues on with our relationship in Jesus Christ. Just as there is one God the Father, there is one Lord Jesus Christ. By Christ, all things that were created continually consist. Notice the difference between *"we in him,"* and *"we by him."* We have a relationship in God the Father, by Jesus Christ. While Paul does not mention the Holy Spirit, as believers, we know the Holy Spirit abides in us. To summarize it in a memorable way; we are in the Father, by the Son, through the Holy Spirit. We have received the Grace of the Father, the Blood of the Son, and the Fruit of the Spirit.

Verse seven says, *"Howbeit there is not in every man that knowledge: for some with conscience of the idol unto this hour eat it as a thing offered unto an idol; and their conscience being weak is defiled."* God wants you to examine your atmosphere wherever you are and whatever state of singleness you may be in. Believers at

---

63

Corinth needed to be mindful of the young babes in Christ who still had weak consciences. When one of them saw a Christian eating food that was sacrificed unto idols, they may have perceived that person was worshiping other gods.

After this progression of teaching, Paul finally reveals a direct answer to the question in verse eight. *"But meat commendeth us not to God: for neither, if we eat, are we better; neither, if we eat not, are we the worse."* For those who knew the idols were nothing, eating of those foods as sacrificed unto them was not sin. Eating it would not bring them closer to God, nor would it carry them further away from God, because they did not worship those gods.

With an <u>answer from God</u> always comes a <u>warning from God</u>. Verse nine says, *"But take heed lest by any means this liberty of yours become a stumblingblock to them that are weak."* As Christians, they had the liberty to make their own decisions. Remember, with liberty comes responsibility. In the same manner, with all decisions come consequences. Sometimes, it is not knowing what is right or wrong, but knowing what is best for the Christian to do. May none of us be stumbling blocks, preventing people from coming to Christ by our actions or words.

Verse ten and eleven says, *"For if any man see thee which hast knowledge sit at meat in the idol's temple, shall not the conscience of him which is weak be emboldened to eat those things which are offered to idols; And through thy knowledge shall the weak brother perish, for whom Christ died?"* According to II Peter 3:9, God does not wish that any man should perish. This should be our same desire. We should care so much for others that we are willing to sacrifice ourselves.

Verse twelve says, *"But when ye sin so against the brethren, and wound their weak conscience, ye sin against Christ."* In this verse we see sin, sorrow, and severity. We must self-limit ourselves in certain situations to avoid becoming stumbling blocks for others.

The chapter ends with verse thirteen; *"Wherefore, if meat make my brother to offend, I will eat no flesh while the world standeth, lest I make my brother to offend."* Paul concludes that we must sacrifice for the sake of our brethren in Christ.

May I add that we must sacrifice for the sake of others. Our sacrifice should not only be for brethren in Christ, but for the lost world who steadily have their eyes fixed in our direction.

Spirit of Sacrifice

What kind of spirit does the Lord require for sacrifice? Psalm fifty-one is one of the few penitential Psalms. Penitential means to be regretful and repentant over sin or wrongdoing. Throughout Psalm fifty-one, we find David in this state of sorrow because of his sin with Bathsheba. Thankfully, all penitential Psalms lead us back to God and his forgiveness.

Psalm 51:16 says, *"For thou desirest not sacrifice; else would I give it: thou delightest not in burn offering."* Imagine the scrutiny that David received because of these very words. This psalm was written in the Old Testament times, meaning that the covenant of animal sacrifice was still upheld. David is not saying that sacrifices and burnt offerings are not important, because there are many times we find him sacrificing to God. What David is saying is that God is more concerned with the <u>heart</u> than the <u>work</u>. While the <u>outward work</u> of sacrifice would be necessary for the written law, God wanted the <u>inward work</u> to take place within the law of his heart.

If God didn't desire the sacrifice of a burnt offering, then what did he desire? Verse seventeen says, *"The sacrifices of God are a broken spirit: a broken and a contrite heart, O God, thou wilt not despise."* We come sacrificing to God with brokenness, but we leave with singleness.

The later end of Acts 13:22 says, *"I have found David the son of Jesse, a man after mine own heart, which shall fulfil all my will."* Originally, God found his way to David's heart. Now, David would have to find his way back to God's heart. When our hearts are aligned with God, our will should be aligned with God. David was not living in the <u>will of God</u>, because he was living in the <u>way of sin</u>.

———

In Psalm 40:6-8, we find this theme expressed in a similar way. *"Sacrifice and offering thou didst not desire; mine ears hast thou opened: burnt offering and sin offering hast thou not required. Then said I, Lo, I come: in the volume of the book it is written of me, I delight to do thy will, O my God: yea, thy law is within my heart."* The key words in this verse are <u>will</u> and <u>heart</u>. In sacrifice, God desires your <u>will and heart</u> over your <u>wood and hands</u>. God's problem with sacrifice was that it was not offered with pure motives, love, or faithfulness to Him. It was not the <u>practice</u> of sacrifice that was Israel's problem, but the <u>pureness</u> in sacrifice.

God affirms His view of sacrifice in Psalm 50:8-12,

"I will not reprove thee for thy sacrifices or thy burn offerings, to have been continually before me. I will take no bullock out of thy house, nor he goats out of thy folds. For every beast of the forest is mine, and the cattle upon a thousand hills. I know all the fowls of the mountains: and the wild beasts of the field are mine. If I were hungry, I would not tell thee: for the world is mine, and the fulness thereof."

The goal in sacrifice is not offering God something he needs, but something He desires; the offering of oneself completely. God needs nothing, for everything is His! Let us not seek to be <u>filled by the flesh</u>, but be <u>filled by faith</u>. God desires for us to be filled from his fullness.

David's plea to God in Psalm 51:10 was, *"create in me a clean heart, O God; and renew a right spirit within me."* David realized the root of the problem; the condition of the heart. The Lord has the power to both clean and renew our inward man.

The chapter concludes with verse nineteen, *"Then shalt thou be pleased with the sacrifices of righteousness, with burnt offering and whole burnt offering: then shall they offer bullocks upon thine altar."* It is only after your heart has been cleaned and your spirit has been renewed that God will accept your sacrifice.

Acts 7:41 says, *"And they made a calf in those days, and offered sacrifice unto the idol, and rejoiced in the works of their own hands."* Remember, God desires the sacrifice of heart over the sacrifice of hands. This is the sound spirit of sacrifice!

Selflessness in Sacrifice

The most selfless man to ever exist, and that ever will exist, is Jesus Christ. Hebrews 10:1 says, *"For the law having a shadow of good things to come, and not the very image of the things, can never with those sacrifices which they offered year by year continually make the comers thereunto perfect."* The first covenant between God and man was only temporary. The Mosaic law, in which sacrifice was put into order, was only a shadow of the good thing that was to come. While God made animal sacrifice <u>essential</u>, he didn't make it <u>eternal</u>. Day by day, month by month, year by year they offered up sacrifices that would never be able to make them complete.

Jesus Christ was the *"image"* that the previous verse spoke of. The law was the shadow, while Christ was the image of that shadow. Hebrews 10:5-6 says, *"Wherefore when he cometh into the world, he saith, Sacrifice and offering thou wouldest not, but a body hast thou prepared me: In burnt offerings and sacrifices for sin thou hast had no pleasure."* Jesus portrayed selflessness just to come down to this world on our behalf. Notice how He described sacrifice when He came to this earth. *"In burnt offerings and sacrifices for sin thou had no pleasure."* It sounds almost exactly how David had described it several thousand years before in Psalms 51. Paul came to God with a <u>broken heart</u> for sacrifice, whereas Christ would come with a <u>broken body</u> for sacrifice.

The Word continues in verse seven, *"Then said I, Lo, I come (in the volume of the book it is written of me,) to do thy will, O God."* Jesus portrayed selflessness just to do God's will. Pay attention to how closely this correlates with what David said in Psalm 40:7, *"then said I, Lo, I come: in the volume of the book it is written of me."* There is no doubt that God, through inspiration, allowed this to happen. I believe this shows us the omniscience of God, but also allows us to see the affirmation of David's heart.

Whenever you have the heart of God, you will think, talk and walk like Him. Both Jesus and David sought to fulfill the will of the Father.

The contrast of sacrifice is revealed in Hebrews 10:11-12, *"And every priest standeth daily ministering and offering oftentimes the same sacrifices, which can never take away sins: But this man, after he had offered one sacrifice for sins for ever, sat down on the right hand of God;"* Jesus portrayed selflessness in the sacrifice of himself. Verse eleven begins with the insufficiency of the sacrifice of man's hands to forgive sins. Any time we see the word but in scripture, we can be thankful that God doesn't end on the negative note. *"But this man,"* Jesus Christ, *"offered one sacrifice for sins forever,"* through the body he was given. He sat down because his work was done. Understand the contrast between the priests and the High Priest. They stood, He sat. They offered daily, He offered once.

Hebrews 10:16-18 reveals the contrast of the covenants. *"This is the covenant that I will make with them after those days, saith the Lord, I will put my laws into their hearts, and in their minds will I write them: And their sins and iniquities will I remember no more. Now where remission of these is, there is no more offering for sin."* Notice the difference between the two covenants. Hebrews 10:3 says, *"But in those sacrifices there is a remembrance again made of sins every year."* In the first covenant there was remembrance of sin, but in the second covenant God will *"remember no more."* In the first covenant there were sacrifices made for sin, but in the second covenant *"there is no more offering for sin."* In the first covenant, God wrote the laws on stone, but in the second covenant he would *"put [his] laws into their hearts, and in their minds will [he] write them."* The Bible says in verse nine, *"He taketh away the first, that he may establish the second."* Jesus Christ came selflessly to fulfill the law.

Hebrews 13:15-16 summarizes sacrifice. *"By him therefore let us offer the sacrifice of praise to God continually, that is, the fruit of our lips giving thanks to his name. But to do good and to communicate forget not: for with such sacrifices God is well pleased."* Selfless sacrifice is the giving of ourselves. May we give God what he truly desires; praise!

The more I read the word of God, the more I see why David was described as being a man after God's own heart. David realized his sin. David repented of his sin. David knew what pleased God. David sought not to displease God. David understood sacrifice. David gave God praise.

I strongly encourage you to read through the book of Psalms. The heart is referenced 132 times throughout the entire book. Many different issues of the heart are dealt with. Before writing "Seeking Singleness," I read through the entire book of Psalms. I cannot begin to tell you how the Lord spoke to my life. You must do more than simply read the words, you must meditate upon them. Reading the Psalms will complete your understanding of what is written in this book. It will help you to search out your heart for God. Remember, you cannot seek singleness without seeking a heart for God.

Here are my "Three P's of the Heart" that you must have in order to sacrifice in singleness: Preparation of the heart, Practice with the heart, and Praise from the heart. In singleness, being a sincere, surrendered, selfless, separated servant is going to take sacrifice.

Take this time to answer the questions for Chapters 7-9 on the self-evaluation page of the beginning of this book.

Chapter 10:
Satisfaction in Singleness

I believe that single people are so busy <u>searching</u> in singleness, that they cannot be <u>satisfied</u> with their singleness. Seeking is to <u>aim</u> at something with intentions to <u>gain</u>. Searching is to look over thoroughly in an effort to <u>unwind</u> to <u>find</u>.

I often substitute these words for one another, but I believe there is a deeper meaning between them. If I am <u>searching</u> for something, then that means I am doing everything in my power to find it. I am looking thoroughly and I am not going to give up until it is found. I will do everything in my power to make it my possession as quickly as possible. Searching implies that something is misplaced; it is a need and I cannot live without it. On the other hand, if I am seeking something, then I am simply setting aim at it. It is not necessarily a need, but it is a desire. I have an <u>aim</u> towards something and my intentions are to one day <u>gain</u> it.

I believe that many people think that in order to be satisfied in singleness, you must only have self-love. Satisfaction doesn't come from self-love. The majority of young people say that if you have enough likes on social media, then you will be satisfied with yourself. Satisfaction doesn't come from social media. Others claim that if you talk to enough people on snapchat, then you will be satisfied in your singleness. Satisfaction doesn't come from snapchat. These are people who are <u>searching</u> rather than <u>seeking</u>.

In *The Christian Home*, written by Clarence Sexton, he says,

> *"All mankind is searching for security… we are also searching for satisfaction. When we take significance, security, and satisfaction, and apply the search for these to the old nature, we see how wild people can become in their searching and how far off course they can go trying to find these things."*

How does a person who has never been in a relationship find satisfaction in his singleness? How does a widow who had been married for 20 years find satisfaction in her singleness? How does a broken-hearted teenager find satisfaction in her singleness? How does a Bible College student find satisfaction in his singleness? You find satisfaction in singleness by being satisfied with the Savior. You must stop searching and start seeking.

Satisfied with His Sufficiency

Being satisfied with the Savior means you believe Christ is sufficient to fill your every need. Now here is my question; if you believe God is sufficient enough to cover your sin, why don't you believe he is sufficient enough to satisfy your singleness?

In II Corinthians 12:9, Jesus says, *"My grace is sufficient for thee: for my strength is made perfect in weakness."* God's grace is indeed sufficient. The strength of God is made perfect, or complete, in our weakness. Do not think that I am saying being single is a weakness, because it is not. Even if you believe that your singleness is your weakness, then Christ can make it complete through His strength!

Satisfaction with the Savior does not come by the sufficiency of self. II Corinthians 3:5 says, *"Not that we are sufficient of ourselves to think any thing as of ourselves; but our sufficiency is in God."* As Christians, we believe that Christ, and He alone, satisfies. He does not just have the answers to singleness; He is the answer to singleness. When you have Him, you have everything you need to live a satisfied, sufficient life.

Ironically, your satisfaction in singleness will come from your relationship with the Lord. You should be satisfied in your relationship with Christ, but never satisfied with your relationship with Christ. What I mean by this is that we should be satisfied knowing that Christ is sufficient, but we should not let our satisfaction become slackness. You can always be satisfied where God is, but you should never be satisfied where you are… this is what causes men to become slack. Even though we have all of the Holy Spirit indwelling our body, we should always strive to grow

72

closer to Him. Don't take for granted your relationship with the Lord. Remember, singleness is about your nearness to God, not your distance from the opposite sex.

If God is sufficient for salvation then He is sufficient for singleness.

Satisfied by Your Sin

Sin may satisfy the soul, but it does not satisfy the spirit. The Bible tells us in Hebrews 11:25, Moses *"[chose] rather to suffer affliction with the people of God, than to enjoy the pleasure of sin for a season."* As we have seen in the life of David, the pleasure of sin only lasts but for a season. As we saw in the garden of Eden, the promises of Satan are always deceptive. As we have seen in our own lives, the product of sin is death.

James 1:14-15 says, *"But every man is tempted, when he is drawn away of his own lust, and enticed. Then when lust hath conceived, it bringeth forth sin: and sin, when it is finished, bringeth forth death."* We can reflect upon the sin of David with Bathsheba in II Samuel chapter eleven, and see the downward slope of sin.

1. *"But David tarried still at Jerusalem."* When David tarried, he was tempted.
2. *"And from the roof he saw a woman washing herself."* When he was tempted, he was drawn away from his own lust.
3. *"And the woman was very beautiful to look upon."* When he was drawn away from his own lust, he was enticed.
4. *"And David sent and enquired after the woman."* When he was enticed, he enquired.
5. *"And David sent messengers, and took her, and she came in unto him, and he lay with her."* When he enquired, his lust conceived.
6. *"And the woman conceived, and sent and told David, and said, I am with child."* When his lust was conceived, his child was conceived.

David was never able to be satisfied with sin. He thought he could have self-control over sin, but before long the sin had control over him. The same stands true to your life. That sin of lust will soon develop in to the sin of pornography. That sin of pornography will develop into the sin of masturbation. That sin of masturbation will develop into the sin of fornication. That sin of fornication will develop into the sin of adultery.

Don't look at where you fell because of sin, look at where you first slipped. You didn't begin to fall when you first <u>sinned</u>, you began to fall when you first <u>slipped</u>. The slip is what caused you to fall; therefore, your slackness with God was what caused you to sin.

Just like David, you will never be satisfied with your sin. Remember that satisfaction of sin leads to sorrow of sin. Sorrow of sin then leads to the scars of sin. We can prevent both sorrow and scars if we will be satisfied with the Savior rather than sin. David was so busy searching, that he forgot to seek.

Satisfied with Your State

"Art thou bound unto a wife? Seek not to be loosed" (I Corinthians 7:27). Are you married? Stop searching. Are you engaged? Stop searching. Are you in a relationship? Stop searching. God gave us the record of David's sin, so that we would not have to fall into the same sin. The Lord wants you to be satisfied in the state that you are in. <u>Seek</u> for <u>Him</u>, don't <u>search</u> for <u>sin</u>.

"Art thou loosed from a wife? Seek not a wife." (I Corinthians 7:27). Are you a single young person? Stop searching. Are you a widow or widower? Stop searching. Are you a virgin? Stop searching. Use the time of your single state to seek God's call in your life and follow His will. Be <u>willing</u> where you are called. Be <u>working</u> where you are called. Be <u>worshiping</u> where you are called.

I have known friends who cannot go without a boyfriend or girlfriend. As soon as one relationship fails, they are already working on another one. "Seeking singleness" is using the time God has blessed you with to surrender, serve, and sacrifice to Him. One of the most important aspects of singleness is time. Take time to be single. Don't spend your singleness searching for "the one," spend your singleness seeking "The One" (Jesus Christ). When you seek "The One," He will send the one (a life-mate). The Lord knows your needs and He desires to fill your needs.

When we stop searching, we can start seeking. When we start "seeking singleness," we can be satisfied.

Chapter 11:
Solution to Singleness

The solution to singleness is in "seeking singleness." The solution to "seeking singleness" is to seek the Savior. The solution to any situation will always be Jesus Christ. We find three C's that solve the situation of singleness.

Contentment with Christ

Philippians 4:11-13 says,

"Not that I speak in respect of want: for I have learned, in whatsoever state I am, therewith to be content. I know both how to be abased, and I know how to abound: every where and in all things I am instructed to be full and to be hungry, both to abound and to suffer need. For I can do all things through Christ which strengtheneth me."

The solution to singleness is your contentment with Christ! Paul first says, *"for I have learned."* We learn most in our life by personal experience. Paul said *"for I have learned, in whatsoever state I am, therewith to be content."* Paul learned from personal experience how to be content with the state that God had him in.

He continued to say, *"I know both how to be abased, and I know how to abound."* The word abased means to be in a low or humble state. The word abound means to be in a well accommodated or higher state. Paul claims from personal experience, he has been both in the lowest of lows and the highest of highs.

He goes a step further by saying, *"every where and in all things I am instructed to be full and to be hungry."* Paul not only had to learn how to be content in his state, but he had to learn to be content everywhere he was led, and in all things that he did. How are we to be both full and hungry at the same time? My high school English teacher would have called this sentence a paradox because of the contradiction between the two ideas of being both full and hungry. When we look at it through spiritual eyes, we can be full in our contentment with Christ, while also being hungry to grow closer to Him. God is the One who fills us, but we are the ones who must show thirst and hunger for Him to do so.

Everyone knows Philippians 4:13, but I hope you see the importance of its preceding verses. You can do all things through Christ, because He strengthens you. You can remain single with the strength of the Lord. You can give your time and talents to Him. You can build your relationship with God. You can be content with Christ.

Are you single? Be content. Are you a widow or widower? Be content. Are you in a relationship? Be content. Are you a virgin? Be content. Are you married? Be content. Are you divorced? Be content.

Whatever state you are in, be content in Christ. Paul is the perfect example of contentment for single Christians. He learned through experience of the ups and downs how to live a life of singleness to God.

Commitment to Christ

Your <u>contentment</u> in Christ will reflect through your <u>commitment</u> to Christ. David learned the importance of commitment to Christ, even after he had committed sin.

Proverbs 16:9 says, *"a man's heart deviseth his way: but the LORD directeth his steps."* Just as David, your natural heart desires sin. You always want to go <u>your</u> way, but when you commit to the Lord, you are committing to follow <u>His</u> way.

In Psalm 37:4-5, David writes, *"Delight thyself also in the LORD: and he shall give thee the desires of thine heart. <u>Commit</u> thy way unto the LORD; trust also in him; and he shall bring it to pass."* If you commit your way unto the Lord, trust in Him, and align your heart with His, then He will give you the desires of our heart. The desires of your heart should not be for the things that you want, but the things that He would want for you.

Proverbs 16:3 says, *"Commit thy works unto the LORD, and thy thoughts shall be established."* Not only are you to commit your ways to the Lord, but you are to commit your works to the Lord. If you have the right way, then you will have the right work.

Commitment to Christ is a very serious step. If you do not commit, then you will not be content. If you are not content, then you will not commit. Commit your way and your work to the Lord.

Comfort in Christ

I think back to Psalm 69:20 when David said, *"Reproach hath broken my heart; and I am full of heaviness: and I looked for some to take pity, but there was none; and for comforters, but I found none."* Do you know why David couldn't find comfort? He was searching for comforters rather than seeking the Comforter. He was looking for pity more than progress. Whenever you need comfort, you must always look to God first. David would soon realize where his true comfort came from; God. *"Thou shalt increase my greatness, and comfort me on every side"* (Psalm 71:21).

II Corinthians 1:3-4 says, *"Blessed be God, even the Father of our Lord Jesus Christ, the Father of mercies, and the God of all comfort; Who comforteth us in all our tribulation, that we may be able to comfort them which are in any trouble, by the comfort wherewith we ourselves are comforted of God."* Christ is the source of your comfort. He is the *"God of all comfort."* He can comfort you in your singleness. He can comfort you after you sin. He can comfort you through your scars. He can comfort you in your solitude. He can comfort you in your sorrow.

God will *"[comfort] us in all our tribulation, that we may be able to comfort them which are in any trouble."* Many times, God allows you to find comfort in other Christians. How does He use other Christians to comfort those in trouble? *"By the comfort wherewith we ourselves are comforted of God."* The reason

Christians can <u>give</u> comfort is because they have been <u>given</u> comfort in Christ! Always remember that when God sends you Christian comforters, he first sent comfort to them in their trouble. It is not what man is giving you, but what God has given that man to give you.

I hope this book will help you find comfort in Christ. I wrote it for that very reason; to comfort others where Christ has comforted me. My goal was to make "Seeking Singleness" more about the Bible and what God's Word had to say, than a book with what words I wanted to say. When you look for comforters in the world, you will find none. When you look for comfort in the Lord, you will find it.

Take this time to answer the questions for Chapters 10-11 on the self-evaluation page of the beginning of this book.

Summarizing Singleness

God burdened me many years ago with the issue of singleness. I struggled being single. I struggled with sin. I struggled with sorrow. I struggled with scars. I struggled with solitude. I struggled with surety. I struggled with sincerity. I struggled in surrendering. I struggled in servanthood. I struggled in sacrifice. I struggled in satisfaction. I struggled with a solution. Once I began to seek singleness in heart with God, I found comfort in Christ.

You do not have to be single to seek singleness!

Psalm 104:4 says, *"Seek the LORD, and his strength: seek his face forevermore."* In whatever state you are in, *"Seek the LORD."* If you want the strength of the Lord, you must *"seek his face forever more."* When you start seeking, don't stop!

Psalm 119:2 says, *"Blessed are they that keep his testimonies, and that seek him with the whole heart."* I hope that you understand the importance of both the condition and character of your heart. Seeking singleness is seeking God with your whole heart.

I pray that God blesses these words more than I can imagine. I pray that he reveals His <u>will</u> to you. I pray that he reveals His <u>way</u> to you. I pray that he reveals His <u>work</u> to you.

If you want to seek singleness, you must be willing to give your whole heart to God. If you are willing to give your whole heart to God, then let this be your prayer:

> "Search me, O God, and know my heart: try me, and know my thoughts: And see if there be any wicked way in me, and lead me in the way everlasting" (Psalm 139:23-24).

Let Him <u>search</u> you, while you <u>seek</u> Him.

Once you have sincerely started "Seeking Singleness," you may soon be "Ready for a Relationship" ...

Self-Evaluation of Singleness

Now that you have read through all of the chapters, reflect upon your heart and answer the follow question (there is no right or wrong answer. This is about what you got from the book):

Summarizing Singleness:

1. What does "Seeking Singleness" mean to you?

I would greatly appreciate feedback on how God used "Seeking Singleness" in your life.

Feel free to contact me any time by means of email:
dylanpowellministries@gmail.com

If you would like to follow the Lord's work in my life, you can do so by following these social media outlets:
Facebook: Dylan Powell Ministries
Instagram: @dylanpowellministries

If you would like me to speak at any church function, revivals, youth conferences, services, special meetings, etc., please contact me by any of the above methods.

Made in the USA
Columbia, SC
21 March 2022